BRITAIN IN OLD PHOTOGRAPHS

LAMBETH,
KENNINGTON
& CLAPHAM

JILL DUDMAN

LAMBETH ARCHIVES DEPARTMENT

SUTTON PUBLISHING

Sutton Publishing Limited
Phoenix Mill · Thrupp · Stroud
Gloucestershire · GL5 2BU
in association with
Lambeth Archives Department

First published 1996

Cover illustrations. Front: rebuilding the road
with tram tracks, Albert Embankment, 1931.
Back: Bishop's Walk, 1866.

British Library Cataloguing in Publication Data
A catalogue record for this book is available from the
British Library.

ISBN 0-7509-1073-9

Typeset in 10/12 Perpetua.
Typesetting and origination by
Sutton Publishing Limited.
Printed in Great Britain by
Ebenezer Baylis, Worcester.

CONTENTS

Introduction   5

1. Lambeth Riverside and North Lambeth   7

2. Vauxhall and South Lambeth   43

3. Kennington   57

4. Stockwell   85

5. Clapham   107

Acknowledgements   126

The parish church of St Mary, Lambeth, with Lambeth Palace behind, viewed from the end of Lower Fore Street, *c.* 1866. This street was swept away by the construction of the Albert Embankment, but it may be located in the map on page 8.

INTRODUCTION

This book aims to give a visual impression of the northern and western parts of the borough of Lambeth as they appeared in the late nineteenth and early twentieth centuries. Starting from the riverside area at the northern end, historically known as Lambeth (as distinct from the much greater extent of the modern borough), the districts covered include also Vauxhall, South Lambeth, Kennington, Stockwell and Clapham. Strictly speaking, the last-mentioned of these is an odd one out, since only with the local government reorganization of 1964 did Clapham become part of Lambeth, having always previously been in Wandsworth. The photographs range in date through several generations from the mid-1860s to the Second World War. This book, along with *Brixton and Norwood in Old Photographs* (1995) and *Streatham in Old Photographs* (1993), completes the coverage in this series of the borough of Lambeth.

The origins and development of these areas are too diverse for more than the briefest outline to be given here. The old village of Lambeth, around the parish church of St Mary, existed in the eleventh century. Just to the north was a marshy area where development started around 1800. Many industries – including potteries, barge and boat building, brewing, timber-yards and sawmills, engineering, glass making, and soap boiling – grew up close to the river, which provided both a water supply and a means of transport. Vauxhall was especially famous in the eighteenth century for one of London's most popular leisure resorts, Vauxhall Gardens. South Lambeth, too, attracted visitors in the mid-seventeenth century to the Botanic garden and museum of the Tradescant family. Much of the Kennington area has been a part of the Duchy of Cornwall since the manor was given to a Prince of Wales in the fourteenth century, a factor which has considerably influenced its development. Stockwell, growing from a centre around the old Stockwell Green, is largely a Victorian suburb. Clapham began to be settled by wealthy City merchants in the eighteenth century, with fine large houses being built there. Through the east and south of the region runs the straight line of Kennington Park Road and Clapham Road, following the old Roman Stane Street – a line also followed at the end of the nineteenth century by the electric underground railway.

In these photographs can be seen busy shopping streets, quiet residential roads, industrial buildings, riverside views and attractive parklands. Varying styles of dress and modes of transport make a fascinating study. Buses, trams, commercial and private vehicles, variously horse-drawn, engine-driven or electrified, all appear. Individual views of hospitals, churches, railway stations, theatres, pubs, schools and colleges are also included, as well as such nationally known institutions as Lambeth Palace and the Oval cricket ground.

The outstanding views of riverside industries, buildings and people of old Lambeth (see Section One) are the work of the photographer (and artist) William Strudwick. Working from a base in Newington, he captured a series of vivid images in the mid-1860s prior to and during the construction of the Albert Embankment, which swept away whole streets of slum housing and industrial premises and transformed the district. Lambeth Archives Department owns a set of some eighty of Strudwick's photographs (including views of other parts of Lambeth) thanks to the generosity of Charles Woolley, a former alderman of the borough. Woolley, a keen historian, amassed a collection not only of Strudwick photographs but also of prints, books, maps, glassware and stoneware, with a meticulously detailed catalogue, which he donated to Lambeth in 1915 in the hope that it would form the basis of a borough museum.

The majority of the pictures used in Sections Two to Five are the work of another single photographic firm, R.J. Johns & Co. (later Maycock & Johns). Established in 1911 and working from a base in Tooting, this firm produced over a couple of decades about 12,000 views of districts of London, chiefly south and west, for use as postcards. A few years ago a collection of about 6,000 glass-plate negatives taken by this firm came to light, having been stored in the loft of a house in Mitcham for about fifty years. They were sold by the owner variously to the archives departments of Lambeth, Wandsworth, Merton and Sutton, and to two private collectors in south London. The set acquired by Lambeth Archives, along with prints made by one of these private collectors, Sid Hayden, from some of his plates and supplied to Lambeth, have been drawn on extensively here. Each of these pictures bears a serial number, a caption (always in the same handwriting) describing the location, and the name 'Johns'.

Selections have also been made from various other collections at Lambeth Archives, notably a few wartime scenes taken from Lambeth's Civil Defence albums, and a number of interesting postcard views supplied to Lambeth by another private collector, Ron Elam.

It should be borne in mind that, except where a precisely dated event is depicted, most of the dates given to the photographs are estimates with varying degrees of certainty. Shopping scenes can often be dated with reasonable accuracy by comparison with contemporary street directories, and it has been assumed that groups of pictures with closely related serial numbers were taken at about the same time. The book has been divided into sections corresponding to reasonably distinguishable districts, although it has sometimes been difficult to decide exactly where the boundaries should be drawn. Each section has been arranged as one or more circular tours around the district. Section One starts with the pre-Embankment views, and a map has been included to assist in locating the old streets.

If you have enjoyed this book, why not take it out with you and walk around the streets and parks shown in these views and look to see how much or how little each location has changed? If you would like to take a deeper interest in the local history or environment of your area, there is sure to be a local amenity society which you could join. The region covered in this book falls variously into the areas of the Vauxhall Society, the Brixton Society and the Clapham Society, all of whom have regular meetings and publish newsletters and books. Their addresses, as well as any other information about the material in this book, may be obtained from Lambeth Archives Department, Minet Library, 52 Knatchbull Road, London SE5 9QY, tel: 0171 926 6076.

LAMBETH RIVERSIDE AND NORTH LAMBETH

*The White Hart public house, on the corner of Belvedere
Road and College Street (the latter now vanished),
1898. The Jubilee Gardens now cover this site.*

Detail from Stanford's library map of London and its suburbs, 1862.

The parish church of St Mary Lambeth, *c.* 1866. The massive lamp-posts have long since gone. The notice board on the gate pillar advertises 'Lambeth Cemetery, Tooting, Surrey', the successor to the old parish burial ground.

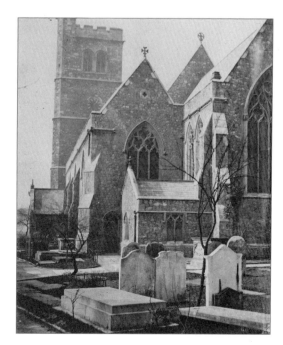

St Mary's Church and churchyard, 1866. The oldest surviving part is the late fourteenth-century tower, the rest of the church having been rebuilt in 1851. Sir Henry Doulton gave a terracotta reredos by his sculptor George Tinworth, the leading sculptor employed by his firm, in 1889. War-damaged, the church ceased to be used in 1972 and became derelict. The Tradescant Trust, founded to rescue it, has now restored the building as the Museum of Garden History. The churchyard, containing the tomb of the Tradescant family of botanists (*see* p. 55) and the Coade stone tomb of Admiral Bligh of *Bounty* fame, is now a garden.

Old houses and shops in Church Street (later renamed Lambeth Road), opposite St Mary's Church, *c.* 1866. The house with the open archway (leading into Swan Yard) was known as Bunyan's Hall, through some supposed connection with John Bunyan. At various times it was used as a Sunday school and a working men's club.

The river shore beside Lambeth Bridge, showing the rear of buildings in Lower Fore Street, *c.* 1866. Here was Henry Doulton's first factory independent of his father's firm, making drainpipes. Wentzell and Edward Wyld were well-known boat builders, and Wyld's was the boat-house for Westminster School.

Swan Yard, off Ferry Street, looking towards the tower of St Mary's Church, *c*. 1866. At the end is the wood-faced rear of the row of houses seen on the opposite page, and in the far left corner is the opening through to Church Street.

Lower Fore Street, looking past the corner of Ferry Street at the left, *c.* 1866. The building on the left was Janeway's pottery. Note its high cellar traps to keep water out – flooding was commonplace here. The large house on the right with lamp and railings was once the Bishop of Hereford's palace.

The river shore, showing the rear of premises in Lower Fore Street, 1866. The gently sloping sandy beach at Lambeth was ideal for building and keeping boats and barges. Robert Bain was another well-known name in the trade.

The river shore, showing the rear of buildings in Upper Fore Street, c. 1866. In some cases, three families shared one house here. The unsanitary conditions are apparent from various small openings in the walls which served to discharge sewage directly on to the open beach.

The river shore, showing the rear of premises in Upper Fore Street, *c.* 1866. This was Smith's pottery, which made drainpipes and other articles. The view gives an idea of working conditions, and shows that boys as young as eleven and twelve were employed.

York Wharf, off Upper Fore Street, *c.* 1866. Most of the residents of these houses were in occupations related to the river, especially fishermen, barge builders, and so on.

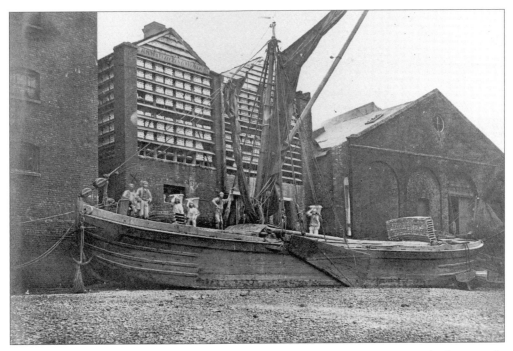

The river shore, showing the rear of premises in Upper Fore Street, 1866. In James Cann's whiting works chalk was washed and crushed to make whiting, which was used by householders for whitewashing walls and keeping the front steps white. His boat was described as a small, stumpy-rigged, flat-bottomed, tiller-steered sailing barge.

An old passageway off Upper Fore Street, *c*. 1866. The darkness prevailing at ground level around the boy contrasts markedly with the sunlight above.

Upper Fore Street, *c.* 1866. The barrels are labelled 'AH', which suggests that this was Alfred Hunt's soap works. Soap was made by boiling bones, a process which produced noxious fumes.

Upper Fore Street, c. 1866. This view is a short distance along from that on the opposite page. The building with the wooden gratings was a whiting storehouse.

Princes Street, photographed from the southern end, *c.* 1866. The building on the left, decorated with urns on top of the frontage, was Cliff's Imperial Potteries. In the distance was the South London Soap Works.

Princes Street, near the corner of Salamanca Street, *c.* 1866. The strong and impervious salt-glazed stoneware made by Lambeth potters such as Henry Millichamp was ideal for drainpipes.

Princes Street, *c.* 1866. The Red Cow public house stood not far from the view shown in the previous photograph, but on the other side of the street.

Construction of the Albert Embankment, looking north towards Lambeth Palace, *c.* 1867. The opportunity was taken to straighten the line of the river bank by excavating a curve of land that projected into the river. Lower and Upper Fore Streets and most of Princes Street thus vanished.

The river shore, Bishop's Walk, showing Lambeth Pier and Lambeth Palace, 1866. This view was taken shortly before the embankment construction works began. Bishop's Walk was a pedestrian way, hence the row of posts visible across the end by the Palace. In the distance is a separate piece of the Palace's garden on the river side of the path.

The river shore, Bishop's Walk, showing Lambeth Pier, Lambeth Palace and St Mary's Church, *c.* 1866. The passenger steamboat *Dahlia* is at the pier. On the old river wall is an advertising slogan for a fireproof safe dealer.

Lambeth Bridge, looking from Westminster towards the Lambeth side, 1866. This original suspension bridge, opened in 1862, replaced a ferry. It was quite narrow, and owing to deterioration by rusting it was restricted to pedestrian use from 1910. Lambeth Palace can just be seen in the distance.

Bishop's Walk, looking from the northern end, 1866. The premises here included those of the boat builder Searle and the wood carver and picture framer Rorke. At the left is the garden wall of Lambeth Palace, while the wall on the right seems to have some graffiti. In the embankment construction works, this path was turned into part of Palace Road.

Two views of the river shore, showing the rear of premises in Bishop's Walk, *c.* 1865. In the top photograph much activity can be seen in the boat building yards of Nash & Miller, and Renshaw (late Roberts). On the right is the riverside piece of garden belonging to Lambeth Palace. The lower photograph shows the 'hards': planks were driven into the mud to retain the shingle and prevent it from being washed out with the tide, thereby providing a reasonably solid surface for the boats.

Old dock, Stangate, *c.* 1866.

Construction of the Albert Embankment near Stangate, looking south towards Lambeth Bridge, *c.* 1867.
The work included straightening the line of the river bank by reclaiming land from a wider part of the
river. On this reclaimed strip, at the left of the view, St Thomas's Hospital was built. In the foreground are
the steps leading down to the foot of Westminster Bridge.

Stangate, *c.* 1866. The premises on the right, covered in advertisements for a variety of periodicals, belonged to William Cook, bootmaker, tobacconist and newsagent. The wooden house was a general store and greengrocery, owned by Mrs Thompson.

Palace Road (later renamed Lambeth Palace Road), with the corner of Paris Street on the right, 1866. The buildings on the left side, including the Mitre Tavern, North's slate works, several building firms and the Stangate saw mills, were demolished to make way for the construction of St Thomas's Hospital.

Palace Road, photographed from the Westminster Bridge Road end, 1867. Searle & Sons, boat builders, were clearly proud of their royal connections. They originally had premises on the river shore at Stangate and Bishop's Walk, and housed both the royal state barge and Emperor Napoleon III's barge. Next door were the Assembly Rooms where Henry Wilcocke, teacher of dancing, held events. This location was unaffected by the 1860s construction works, but in the 1960s Lambeth Palace Road was diverted along a new line further east, and whole streets were demolished to allow a major expansion of St Thomas's Hospital. The row of buildings seen here, though, had already gone with an earlier road-widening.

St Thomas's Hospital, looking from the junction of Stangate and Westminster Bridge approach, *c*. 1900. Originally an eleventh-century priory at the south end of London Bridge looking after sick travellers, St Thomas's developed in that area until the site was bought up to make way for the railway in 1860. Following a temporary stay elsewhere in Southwark, during which time Florence Nightingale founded the first nursing training school, the new hospital was opened by Queen Victoria in 1871.

Evacuation of patients from St Thomas's Hospital, September 1939. The hospital was severely damaged in the Second World War: it was hit by numerous bombs and incendiaries in 1940–1 and by two V1 flying bombs in 1944. Not a single patient was lost as a result, although ten staff members were killed. Work carried on despite the conditions, and an emergency operating theatre was set up in the basement, where many air-raid casualties were treated.

The south front of the residential wing, Lambeth Palace, *c.* 1866. This London residence of the Archbishops of Canterbury dates from the early thirteenth century, although little survives from that time. There have been numerous additions, such as the Tudor gateway (Morton's Tower), and reconstructions, particularly in the nineteenth century when the chapel and residential wing were rebuilt. The lamp-post has been replaced by a memorial cross.

A garden party was held at Lambeth Palace in June 1945 to mark the standing-down of the Civil Defence services. The crowd was entertained by a band on a makeshift stage. The Palace sustained some bomb damage: the library (in the great hall) and the chapel suffered particularly badly.

Albert Embankment, road works associated with the construction of the new Lambeth Bridge, November 1931. The old bridge was replaced by one more suitable for modern traffic; it opened in 1932. Lambeth Palace and St Mary's Church can be seen in the background.

Albert Embankment, October 1931. The construction of the new Lambeth Bridge involved considerable rebuilding of associated roads, including tram tracks. Watching men at work always seems to be a popular pastime!

Paris Street, off Lambeth Palace Road, 1939. United Dairies were still using horse-drawn milk delivery carts. Paris Street and several other nearby streets disappeared with the expansion of St Thomas's Hospital.

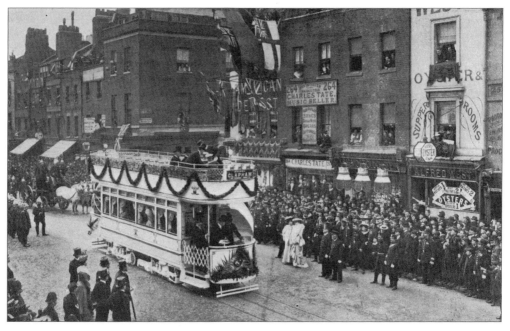

Westminster Bridge Road, near the corner of Belvedere Road, 15 May 1903. The Prince and Princess of Wales, in a specially decorated tram, opened the newly electrified tram route via Clapham to Tooting. The royal passengers each paid half-pennies for their fares and received punched tickets on which Prince of Wales feathers were printed.

The General Lying-In Hospital, York Road, on the corner of Addington Street, *c.* 1905. Originally founded in 1767 in Westminster Bridge Road as a charitable institution for poor women from urban slums in childbirth, the hospital moved to this new building in 1828. The notice on the left made an urgent appeal for funds. The hospital closed in 1971.

The Rising Sun public house, on the corner of York Road and Vine Street, 1898. Vine Street originally ran from the site of Waterloo station, across York Road and Belvedere Road, from where it continued as College Street to the river; it was later renamed Jenkins Street but has since vanished. Note the fine ornamental metalwork on the buildings. This is now approximately the site of the Shell Centre.

Vine Street, corner of York Road, 1898. The wall above this pharmacist's shop displayed a fascinating collection of advertisements for entertainment venues, newspapers, food and drink products and much else.

Jonas Smith & Co.'s moulding works, on the corner of Belvedere Crescent (now vanished) and Vine Street, 1898. Belvedere Crescent was a loop off Belvedere Road, also crossed by Vine Street. This area of industrial and commercial slums, severely damaged in the Second World War, was cleared to make way for part of the Festival of Britain exhibition site in 1951.

The entrance to D. Napier & Son's engineering works, Vine Street, 1898. This major industrial premises, which lay just behind York Road, began work in 1808 and continued until as late as 1958, latterly making cars and aero-engines.

Sufferance Wharf, at the river end of College Street, 1898. This property was typical of the many riverside wharves along this stretch of the river, handling a variety of commodities, in this case corn. The Jubilee Gardens now cover this site.

British American Restaurant, January 1945. Its precise location has not been discovered, but the mural depicting Lambeth Bridge and the entrance to Lambeth Palace suggests that it must have been in the north of the borough. Note the interesting inscription in honour of a female Merchant Navy engineer. Standing, centre, is the Mayor of Lambeth, Alderman W. Lockyer.

North Lambeth riverside, 1938. There is much to be seen in this view. At the extreme left a new Waterloo Bridge was being constructed. The original bridge was opened in 1817 and was given the name Waterloo to commemorate the famous victory (the first use of the name in this area). In the centre was the Shot Tower, dating from 1826, used for making gun-shot by dropping molten lead from the top into a tank of water. At the extreme right was the Lion Brewery, founded in 1837, where a number of artesian wells were drilled to obtain clean water supplies. Surmounting the brewery's frontage was a massive lion figure made of Coade stone. This strong and hard-wearing artificial stone was made locally from 1769 by the Eleanor Coades, mother and daughter, at their factory near College Street. It was a twice-fired clay product with special additives, from which architectural decorative features could be easily and cheaply mass-produced using moulds. Manufacture died out by 1840; knowledge of the correct mix of additives has apparently been lost. This area was also demolished for the Festival of Britain in 1951, except that the Shot Tower was incorporated in the exhibition site next to the Royal Festival Hall and survived until the 1960s, and the Coade stone lion was preserved and now stands at the end of Westminster Bridge.

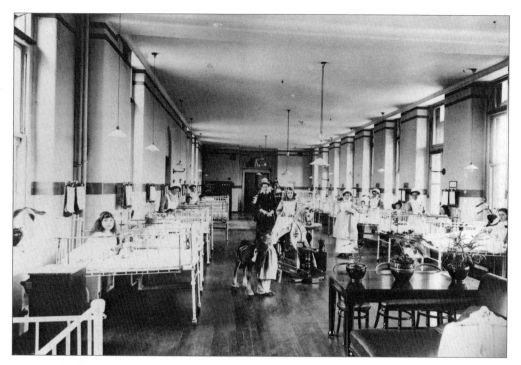

A children's ward, Royal Waterloo Hospital for Children and Women, 1913. Standing on the corner of Waterloo Road and Stamford Street, this hospital dated from 1823 but was rebuilt in 1905, with Doulton glazed tile and terracotta facing incorporating Art Nouveau-style decoration. The hospital closed in the 1980s, but the building survives in educational use.

Waterloo station in the late nineteenth century. The London & South Western Railway originally had its terminus at Nine Elms, but in 1848 it extended its line by way of a brick viaduct through Vauxhall (where much dense slum housing was demolished to make way) to this new terminus, which took its name from Waterloo Bridge.

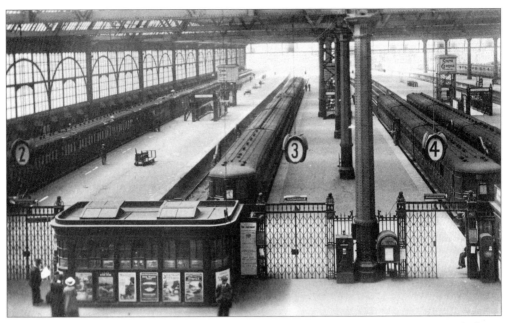

Waterloo station, *c.* 1920. The original station was much enlarged by stages and had twenty-one platforms by 1922, when the frontage was rebuilt to incorporate a memorial to LSWR employees killed in the First World War. This view shows suburban electric trains to Shepperton on Platform 3 and Teddington on Platform 4, the LSWR having introduced 600 volts DC third-rail electrification from 1915.

Waterloo station, 6 May 1939. Amid the decorations, the crowd of VIPs are waving off King George VI and Queen Elizabeth on a lengthy visit to Canada. In the days before air travel was common, royal tours overseas were often made by ocean liner from Southampton: the train from Waterloo was the start of many such journeys.

The Old Vic Theatre, *c.* 1900. A poster on the front advertised Shakespeare, classic plays and operas in English. Opened as the Royal Coburg Theatre in 1818, this establishment saw a major transformation from 1880 as the Royal Victoria Coffee Music Hall directed by Emma Cons. The sale of alcohol was banned and more 'moral' and educational entertainment was put on, including lectures which later developed into Morley College. Miss Cons was succeeded by her niece Lilian Baylis in 1912.

Draper's stall, The Cut, *c.* 1939. This street market, dating from the early nineteenth century and at one time extending along the entire length of The Cut and Lower Marsh, was one of London's largest and most famous. Behind the stallholder can be seen (right to left) the Old Vic Theatre, the corner of Webber Street and the end of a block of shops and buildings that were destroyed in the Second World War.

The Cut, *c.* 1939. Just a short distance along from the previous view, this was also a part of the destroyed block. The notice board outside the Salvation Army hall advertised times of meetings for adults and young people, and offered a hearty invitation and welcome.

Fruit stall, The Cut, *c.* 1939. To modern eyes, the prices here seem remarkable: Brazilian oranges at two for 2½*d*, and bananas 1*d* each.

Clothes stall, Lower Marsh, *c.* 1939.
The reader is left to enjoy this picture
without further comment!

Lower Marsh Infants School, January 1945. Gifts of toys from Melbourne, Australia, were distributed to
young children who had spent almost all their lives in a country at war. Alderman W. Lockyer, Mayor of
Lambeth throughout the Second World War, is in the centre; Mrs Lockyer, the Mayoress is on the right.

Top photograph: Programme of the Royal Canterbury Theatre, c. 1910. Originally a late eighteenth-century tavern, the Canterbury Arms in Upper Marsh was reconstructed about 1850 after the railway viaduct was built over the site, and became one of London's leading music halls. With later extensions the premises became very grand, and included an art gallery and an aquarium. The theatre introduced cinema films from 1912, and was bombed in the Second World War.

Left photograph: Christ Church, at the junction of Westminster Bridge Road and Kennington Road, c. 1900. This church, of the Congregational faith, together with the Hawkstone Hall, was completed in 1876. It was partly funded by branches of the Congregational Church in America, and the spire on the tower (known as the Lincoln Tower) has stars and stripes decoration. Only the tower survives; the remainder, partly war-damaged, was rebuilt in the 1960s and incorporates the Baptist Upton Chapel.

Two views of the Lambeth Baths and Washhouses, at the junction of Lambeth Road and Kennington Road, 1898. This new building had opened in 1897, next to Lambeth Methodist Church (visible on the extreme right of the top photograph). In the days when most of the dwellings in the neighbourhood would have had neither a bath nor hot running water, this public bath and wash-house facility must have been greatly valued. The bottom photograph shows the wash-house, with large sinks on the right and clothes drying racks on the left.

A distant view of Lambeth Baths, photographed from Morton Place across Lambeth Road, 4 January 1945. The devastation caused by a V2 rocket impact, in which the baths were damaged beyond repair, is all too clear.

J.E. Rowling's dairy, on the corner of St Alban's Street and China Walk, *c.* 1900. This firm was founded in 1815 and flourished for over a century. St Alban's Street was a turning off Kennington Road, a short distance behind Lambeth Baths, while China Walk was a turning off Lambeth Road which ran to meet it. The area had been cleared by the 1930s, with blocks of flats built over it.

SECTION TWO

VAUXHALL AND
SOUTH LAMBETH

The Tate Free Library, South Lambeth Road, c. 1922.
This library, one of three given to Lambeth by Sir Henry
Tate, was opened in 1888. The projecting curved porch
with its supporting figures (caryatids) survived until at
least the 1950s.

A gala night in Vauxhall Gardens, 1804. Opened as the Spring Gardens in the 1660s, this was a favourite haunt of Samuel Pepys, but its major development dated from 1728 when Jonathan Tyers became proprietor. A Gothic domed 'orchestra' (i.e. bandstand) was built for concerts, along with pavilions, colonnades and statues among the trees and lawns, all illuminated by thousands of lamps. Supper refreshments were served.

Ascent of the *Royal Victoria* balloon at Vauxhall Gardens, 1849. In the nineteenth century a greater variety of entertainments were introduced. As well as fancy dress and masked balls, there were fireworks, equestrian performances, scenic displays and ballooning. The gardens closed in 1859 and the 12-acre site, on the north side of Kennington Lane between Goding Street and St Oswald's Place, was built over with housing.

Vauxhall Cross, *c.* 1915. This view of the major road junction outside Vauxhall station, where Albert Embankment, Kennington Lane, South Lambeth Road and Wandsworth Road all meet, shows that traffic congestion is nothing new.

South Lambeth Road, looking past the corner of Lawn Lane, *c.* 1922. On the extreme left can be seen a tall mast carrying signals on the railway viaduct. The Park Mansions block dates from the 1890s.

Vauxhall Park, *c.* 1922. This piece of land had been acquired by a developer in the late nineteenth century, the previous large houses on it being demolished. However, Octavia Hill and her colleagues in the Kyrle Society, who campaigned for the provision of public gardens, persuaded Lambeth Vestry to buy it, the cost being shared by the London County Council (LCC). The park was laid out by the Kyrle Society and opened in 1890.

Vauxhall Park, *c.* 1922. The distinguished statesman Henry Fawcett had lived in one of the houses on this site, and in 1893 Sir Henry Doulton gave a statue of Fawcett by the sculptor George Tinworth, as well as a fountain, to the park. The statue (now demolished) of Fawcett seated with an angel standing behind, can just be seen in the distance.

South Lambeth Road, looking past the corner of Miles Street, *c.* 1922. The factory on the left, which belonged to Brand & Co., makers of concentrated beef tea, has been demolished, but St Anne's Church next to it, dating from 1876, survives. The rather austere Coronation Buildings in the distance were replaced by modern housing in the 1980s.

South Lambeth Road, looking past the corner of Wheatsheaf Lane, *c.* 1922. On the extreme right are the imposing entrance gates into Beaufoy & Co.'s vinegar factory. Built in 1810, its architecture was considered to be of high quality for an industrial building. It suffered damage in the Second World War, and manufacture ceased around 1970.

Old South Lambeth Road, *c.* 1922. The original line of South Lambeth Road had a pronounced kink here, and around 1890 a straight length was built to bypass it. The cut off loop was subsequently renamed Old South Lambeth Road.

South Lambeth Road, looking north towards the junction with Old South Lambeth Road, *c.* 1922. In the distance can be seen the block of Victoria Mansions, built in the fork between the old and new roads.

Wilcox Road, *c.* 1922. Originally this road ran right through from South Lambeth Road (where the library was on the corner) to Wandsworth Road. This view was taken from near the South Lambeth Road end, looking past the corner of Kenchester Street.

Wilcox Road, *c.* 1922. This view is further along, looking past the corner of Wheatsheaf Lane on the right. As part of a major housing development in this area in the 1980s, the eastern section of the road has become a pedestrian way, Wilcox Close.

Mawbey Street, *c.* 1922. Originally this street ran through from South Lambeth Road to Hartington Road. Most of it has disappeared in the development of the housing estate, and only a short portion at the western end of the road remains.

Guildford Road, *c.* 1922. The old building of St Barnabas' Church survives, dating from 1850, but the rest of the right hand side in this view has been redeveloped as new housing. Note the BP Union Jack sign on the right, indicating an early service garage.

Stockwell Baptist Church, South Lambeth Road, 1866. Note the two gentlemen in top hats standing on the pavement in front of this newly completed church. On the left is the Lambeth potter James Stiff, who founded and financed the building. On the right, with paper in hand, is the builder William Higgs.

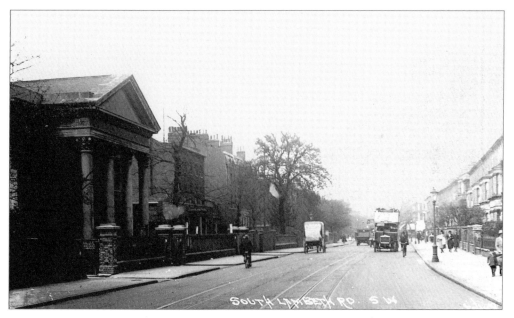

South Lambeth Road, looking past Stockwell Baptist Church, *c.* 1922. This later view, included for comparison, shows quite a difference in the traffic and the state of the roadway.

Portland Place North (later renamed Portland Grove), *c*. 1914. Originally this road had a section leading off Lansdowne Way, and another section at right angles running to meet Clapham Road. Only the former part remains, after a major housing development in this area in the 1960s.

Portland Place South (later renamed Mursell Road), *c*. 1914. This road, now vanished in the development of the housing estate, ran between the surviving section of Portland Place North and Clapham Road, parallel with the other section of Portland Place North.

Clapham Road, looking past the corner of Albert Square, *c.* 1914. The portion of Albert Square which leads out on to Clapham Road had large houses of matching design on both corners, similar to those in the square itself. While the buildings on the other corner survive, the terrace extending from this corner was more badly war-damaged, and was replaced by blocks of flats in the 1960s.

Wilkinson Street, *c.* 1922. On the left can be seen the spire of St Stephen's Church, which was damaged in the Second World War by the cable of a drifting barrage balloon. The church was entirely rebuilt in the 1960s.

St Stephen's Church, South Lambeth, *c.* 1922. The original building, dating from 1861, was of Kentish ragstone.

St Stephen's Terrace, *c.* 1922. This view has also been altered by the rebuilding of the church.

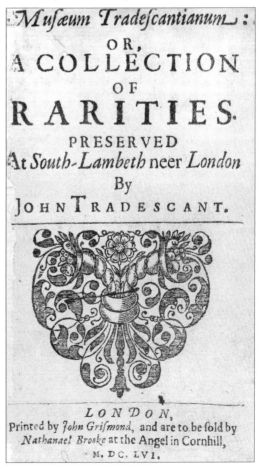

Title page of the catalogue of the Tradescants'
collection, 1656. The John Tradescants, father
and son, were gardeners to King Charles I and
other nobility, and introduced many plant
species collected on their worldwide travels. In
the late 1620s they settled in a house in South
Lambeth Road (near the present Tradescant
Road) where they created a botanic garden. The
house also contained their collection of natural
history and other 'curiosities', known as 'The
Ark', and both garden and museum were open
to the public. The collection was later acquired
by their friend Elias Ashmole, who donated it to
Oxford University to found the Ashmolean
Museum.

Dorset Road, looking west past the junction with Kibworth Street, *c.* 1914. On the right was the Primitive Methodist chapel, directly opposite the Royal William public house. This part of the road was largely rebuilt with blocks of flats in the 1940s.

Dorset Road, looking past the corner of Palfrey Place on the right, *c.* 1914. The Blue House was a well-known laundry. This section of the road, nearer to Clapham Road, was redeveloped with housing in the 1960s.

KENNINGTON

*Imperial Court, Kennington Lane, c. 1930. At this
time the building was the headquarters of the Navy,
Army & Air Force Institutes (NAAFI), caterers to the
armed services. They had taken over from the original
occupier, the Licensed Victuallers' School, in 1921
(see p. 71).*

St Mark's Church, Kennington, *c. 1912*. Completed in 1824, St Mark's is one of a quartet of churches in Lambeth, built with the help of a government grant for expanding urban populations; the others are St Matthew's at Brixton, St Luke's at West Norwood and St John's at Waterloo. They are often known as the 'Waterloo' churches, through a myth that they commemorated the battle victory.

Kennington Park Road, looking past the Oval underground station, *c.* 1922. This was the original station building, dating from the opening of the City & South London Railway, the first electric underground line, in 1890. In the centre is a tram with a trailer car, used around the time of the First World War to increase passenger capacity.

The Oval underground station, *c.* 1936. The line was closed for reconstruction in 1923/4, with tunnels being enlarged and stations modernized. This view shows the resulting building. The dome which housed the original hydraulic lift equipment has disappeared.

Kennington Park Road, looking south at its junction with the curve leading round to Brixton Road, *c.* 1922. Historically, this was approximately the site of a turnpike gate and toll house, removed in 1865 when turnpike trusts were abolished. The name 'Kennington Gate' seems to have persisted for some years, however.

Kennington Park Road, looking towards the corner of Kennington Road, *c.* 1922. This large firm of house furnishers, Hudson & Walker, along with the rest of the row of buildings on this side from the underground station, were replaced by blocks of flats in the 1930s and '40s.

Kennington Park Road, looking past the corner of Kennington Road, *c*. 1922. On the corner was the Horns Tavern, a public house with historic origins. Note, at the right, that road works have always been a feature of the urban landscape.

The Kennington Theatre, Kennington Park Road (next to the park), *c*. 1922. Opened in 1898, this theatre attracted many leading actors to star in its productions. In 1921 it became a cinema, putting on a mixture of films and variety stage acts, but closed in the late 1930s. The building, with an Italian Renaissance frontage in Portland stone, was demolished and replaced by a block of flats in the 1950s.

The Horns Tavern and Assembly Rooms, on the corner of Kennington Road and Kennington Park Road, *c.* 1885. This was a historic public house site and a focal point of the neighbourhood; the court of the Manor of Kennington met at a building here in the eighteenth century, and Surrey Cricket Club was founded here in the nineteenth century.

The Horns Tavern, Assembly Rooms and Hotel, *c.* 1922. This view shows the reconstructed building of 1887. The assembly hall, which was used for exhibitions and lectures, was bombed in the Second World War. The remainder of the building was demolished and replaced by an office block in the 1960s.

Kennington Road, looking from the corner of Kennington Park Road, *c*. 1922. Ashton's were (and still are) a very old-established firm of undertakers.

Kennington Road, looking towards Kennington Green, *c*. 1922. On the right is an LCC school, built in the characteristic style of architecture of the School Board for London, the LCC's predecessor.

Lambeth Vestry Hall (Town Hall), Kennington Road, *c.* 1870. The Lambeth Vestry, forerunner of the Borough Council, had this hall built in 1853. The building was fairly soon found too small; unable to extend it because of the terms of the lease from the Duchy of Cornwall (owners of the manor of Kennington since the fourteenth century), the Council moved to a new Town Hall in Brixton in 1908. The old building was taken over by the Church of England Society for Waifs and Strays (later the Children's Society) and served as their headquarters for many years.

Old houses opposite the side of the Vestry Hall, Kennington Road, *c.* 1870. These were known as the 'plague houses', having been used, when they were still half-complete shells, as a mortuary for victims of the Great Plague.

Kennington Road, looking past the junction with Lower Kennington Lane, *c.* 1922. In the centre another tram with a trailer car passes yet more road works.

Lower Kennington Lane, looking from the junction with Kennington Road, *c.* 1922. Originally the road extending north-east from this point to Newington Butts was named Lower Kennington Lane, while the road extending south-west to Vauxhall Cross was Upper Kennington Lane. The two were combined in 1936 and renumbered as one road.

Looking north at the junction of Kennington Park Road, Lower Kennington Lane and Newington Butts, *c.* 1870. The old church of St Mary Newington, seen in the distance projecting into the line of the roadway, was demolished in 1876, and a new church was built nearby. An opening had just been cut through the building line on the left to make Dante Road, which marked the Lambeth borough boundary.

Upper Kennington Lane, looking from the Kennington Road end, *c.* 1930. Imperial Court can be seen in the distance. The ivory works on the right had a history going back three centuries.

Cardigan Street, *c.* 1930. At the beginning of the twentieth century the Duchy of Cornwall began to take measures to improve the slum dwellings of many of its tenants. Particularly notable is the Georgian style development of small houses in the Cardigan Street/Courtenay Street area, dating from 1913. The architectural decoration incorporates Prince of Wales feathers.

Courtenay Square, *c.* 1930. This view shows the focal point of this attractive Duchy estate.

The Old Tenants' Hostel, on the corner of Sancroft Street and Newburn Street, *c.* 1930. This quadrangle of small flats around a courtyard was opened in 1914 by the Prince of Wales to provide accommodation for elderly tenants of the Duchy. It has recently been taken over by a housing association and renamed Woodstock Court.

King George VI and Queen Elizabeth visited the Duchy of Cornwall estates on 7 March 1940. They are pictured leaving the Old Tenants' Hostel with the Mayor of Lambeth, Alderman W. Lockyer.

The Old Tenants' Hostel, *c.* 1930. A fountain incorporating a figure of Eros can be seen in the centre of the courtyard.

Bomb-site in the area of Kennington Lane and Vauxhall Street, 18 July 1944. With all the people standing around looking down the hole, one hopes that there is not an unexploded bomb at the bottom of it!

The Moffat Institute, Esher Street (later renamed Aveline Street), *c.* 1930. The Institute originated in mission work in a deprived area by the congregation from Claylands Chapel. In a succession of premises, they provided religious and educational classes for children and adults, social meetings, cheap meals, a savings bank and much else. Their first proper building was opened in Vauxhall Street in 1875 by the missionary Robert Moffat and named after him. The Institute moved to this former chapel in 1896. War-damaged and rebuilt in the 1950s, the premises became Alford House youth club.

Upper Kennington Lane, looking towards Imperial Court on the right, *c.* 1922. This view shows a quiet, almost traffic-free scene on this main thoroughfare.

The Licensed Victuallers' School, Upper Kennington Lane, *c.* 1870. Founded in 1803 'for the education, clothing and maintenance of the orphans and other destitute children of members of the Friendly Society of Licensed Victuallers', the school had this new building erected in 1836. After the school moved out of London in 1921, the building was taken over by the NAAFI and named Imperial Court.

Pilgrim glass works, Montford Place, off Kennington Lane, 8 July 1944. The glass kiln can be seen in the wrecked building, but fortunately the gasholder of the gasworks behind survived the bombing. Hayward's pickle factory nearby was also hit.

Cricket at the Oval, *c.* 1870. The oval-shaped roadway was laid out around 1790 on market garden land belonging to the Duchy of Cornwall. After a number of proposals to build on it had failed, the Oval was effectively preserved as an open space by being leased to the Surrey Cricket Club in 1845. At the extreme right can just be seen part of a gasholder of the Phoenix gas works, founded in 1847.

The entrance to the Oval and the Surrey Tavern, *c.* 1922. A small pavilion and a licensed tavern were built in the early years of the club, and at one time there was also a racket court. A much larger new pavilion and the Jacobean-style Surrey Tavern were built in 1897.

The entrance to the Oval, *c.* 1922. This closer view of the old gates reveals a notice stating admission to be 1*s*.

The entrance to the Oval and the Surrey Tavern, *c.* 1936. The old wooden fence around the ground was replaced by a brick wall in 1934, and these new gates were built to commemorate Sir Jack Hobbs. Over the gates in wrought ironwork are the words 'the Hobbs Gates in honour of a great Surrey and England cricketer'. In the Second World War the ground was planned as a prisoner-of-war camp but never used. The Surrey Tavern was rebuilt in the 1960s.

Kennington Park, *c.* 1915. Historically, this was common land used by tenants of the Manor of Kennington for pasturing animals. By the early nineteenth century it was also being used for recreation, political assemblies, election hustings and religious preaching. In 1848 it was the scene of a famous Chartist meeting, when thousands gathered to march to Westminster with a petition for electoral reforms, but were stopped by a large police force.

Kennington Park, *c.* 1915. Several proposals for turning the land into a more orderly and respectable public park, with a local fund-raising effort aided by the government, culminated in the opening of the park in 1854. It was the first dedicated public open space in Lambeth.

Kennington Park, *c.* 1915. On the right, covered by vegetation (cleared since), is the Prince Consort's model dwelling. Originally part of the 1851 Great Exhibition, this was a model block of improved working class dwellings. It was re-erected in the park in 1852, opposite the end of Kennington Road, to serve as a lodge for staff accommodation.

Kennington Park, *c.* 1915. In the centre of the view, behind the lady, can just be seen a drinking fountain which was donated by Felix Slade in 1862. The upper-cast bronze part with a vase and lotus flowers has disappeared, but the large red granite bowl inlaid with Slade's initials and the date survives.

Kennington Park, *c.* 1915. This view shows, as well as the bandstand in the distance, an ornamental terracotta fountain sculpted by George Tinworth and donated by Sir Henry Doulton in 1869. The upper part, a group of figures carrying a cross, seen rather faintly here, has not survived.

Kennington Park, *c.* 1915. The LCC acquired ownership of the park from the Duchy of Cornwall in 1889, and extended it in 1921 by buying land at the south-east corner and demolishing houses. A swimming pool and a children's playground were installed there.

Kennington Park, *c.* 1930. In the newly extended area, a flower garden enclosed by a low brick wall was also laid out, with pathways and pergolas. Lambeth Council took over the park in 1971 and carried out further extensions.

Brixton Road, looking from the northern end opposite the park, *c.* 1912. This view shows the offices and garage of the General Motor Cab Company Ltd.

Brixton Road, looking towards Kennington Park, *c.* 1912. The building on the left was an LCC Tramways sub-station.

Crewdson Road, *c.* 1920. In the distance can be seen the beginnings of that modern phenomenon, the inner-city side street of old houses (no garages) lined with parked cars.

Brixton Road, looking past the corner of South Island Place, *c.* 1920. A few views in this locality have been included, since it is much nearer to Kennington than to Brixton.

Brixton Road, looking past the corner of Chapel Street (later renamed Mowll Street), *c.* 1920. The large motor engineers' premises on the corner had just opened.

South Island Place, *c.* 1920. Very little remains of the original housing in this road, much rebuilding having taken place in the 1960s and '70s.

The Russell Hotel, on the corner of Brixton Road and Holland Street (later renamed Caldwell Street), *c.* 1920. Presumably the children were gathering for some sort of outing.

Holland Street (later renamed Caldwell Street), looking from the Clapham Road end, *c*. 1914. This street has also been largely rebuilt.

Clapham Road, showing the terrace between the corners of South Island Place and Holland (Caldwell) Street, *c*. 1914. Along with the redevelopment of the side streets, this row of large houses on the main road was replaced by new buildings in the 1960s and '70s.

Clapham Road, showing the terrace between the corners of Crewdson Road and South Island Place, *c.* 1914. Much rebuilding has taken place here. The notice for the antiseptic hairdressing salon advertised shaving for 2*d* and haircutting for 3*d*.

Clapham Road, looking past the corner of Richmond (later Richborne) Terrace, *c.* 1914. In the 1920s the London Terminal Coach Station was built, a long narrow structure lying parallel between Richmond Terrace and Fentiman Road, fronting on to Palfrey Place. The middle part of the block in this view was demolished to provide an opening on to Clapham Road. Housing was built on the coach station site in the 1980s.

Richmond Terrace, *c.* 1914. Originally the housing on the north side of this road was named Richmond Terrace, while that on the south side was Osborne Terrace. It must have been confusing to have a street with different names on opposite sides, and by the 1930s the two had been combined into Richborne Terrace. The street lamp had the name of the side turning, Palfrey Place, in its glass.

Clapham Road, showing a row of shops near the northern end, opposite the corner of Prima Road, *c.* 1936. The furniture store was advertising walnut suites for £7 19*s* 6*d*. There was also a coach booking agent here.

Belgrave Hospital for Children, Clapham Road, *c.* 1922. Originally founded in the 1860s in Pimlico (hence the name), the hospital moved to a new building here in 1903. Further wings were added in the 1920s. Notices on the building stated that the hospital was supported by voluntary contributions and that funds were urgently needed. The hospital closed in the 1980s.

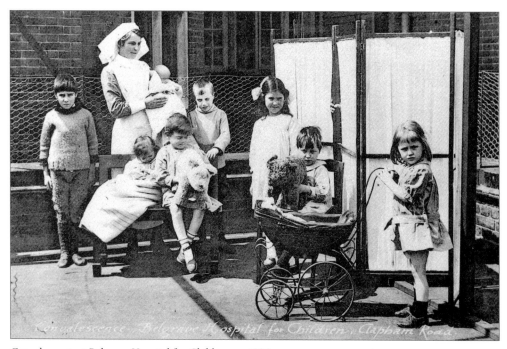

Convalescents at Belgrave Hospital for Children, *c.* 1930.

STOCKWELL

*Stockwell war memorial, c. 1922. This memorial, to
commemorate those who died in the First World War, was
built in the centre of Stockwell's major road junction in
1921.*

The Swan Tavern, on the corner of Stockwell Road and Clapham Road, 1866. Standing on another historic public house site, the building shown here was itself replaced in the 1930s.

Clapham Road, looking past the corner of Binfield Road, *c.* 1922. Prominent in the view is the dome housing the hydraulic lift equipment of the original Stockwell underground station, the terminus of the City & South London Railway when it first opened in 1890.

Clapham Road, looking towards the corner of Binfield Road, *c.* 1912. This close-up view of some of the buildings in the previous scene shows attractive ornamentation. Note the model piano sign on the shop front, and the Sainsbury's delivery bicycles. The London & South Western Bank was later amalgamated into Barclays.

Clapham Road, looking past the corner of Binfield Road, *c.* 1930. Taken from virtually the identical point as the picture opposite, this view shows the 1920s rebuilt underground station. With the coming of the new Victoria Line to Stockwell, the station was rebuilt yet again around 1970 to provide an interchange.

Stockwell war memorial and gardens, *c*. 1922. After the building development of the area, a small triangular piece of open land was left between the junction of South Lambeth Road and Clapham Road. Here the memorial was built and a garden was laid out, which appears to have been an attractive place to sit or stroll at that time, with little motor traffic around.

Crowds gathering at Stockwell war memorial for Remembrance Day, *c*. 1922. The bicycle was still a very popular form of transport.

Clapham Road, looking past the corner of Lansdowne Road (later renamed Lansdowne Way), *c.* 1914. The wine merchant on the corner was advertising Listrac Medoc claret at 16*s* for a dozen bottles.

The printing works of Sir Joseph Causton & Sons Ltd, Clapham Road (near the corner of Durand Gardens), *c.* 1914. On the frontage they advertised themselves as manufacturing stationers, letterpress printers, cheque & bond engravers, account book & envelope makers, and much else. The building was taken over by Freemans as a mail order warehouse in 1937, and greatly extended.

Clapham Road, looking past the corner of Stockwell Park Road, *c.* 1914. Not far from here, the house at 27 Stockwell Park Road carries a Blue Plaque recording that 'Lilian Baylis, 1874–1937, Manager of the Old Vic and Sadler's Wells Theatres, lived and died here'.

Stockwell Park Road, looking south past the corners of Robsart Street and Sidney Road, *c.* 1922. Originally Stockwell Park Road continued more or less straight from this point to join Brixton Road. Its line has been much altered by the development of a housing estate over the area in the 1970s.

Stockwell Park Crescent, *c.* 1922. Against the background of these 1840s houses can be seen a problem of bicycle travel: the need to stop and repair a puncture.

Stockwell Park Road, 22 June 1944. Although damaged, St Michael's Church, dating from 1841, stands proudly among the wreckage of a V1 flying bomb impact.

The British & Foreign School Society's Training College for Mistresses, Stockwell Road (near the corner of St Michael's Road), *c.* 1922. The BFSS was founded in the early nineteenth century to set up schools and teacher training colleges based on non-sectarian Christian principles, both in Britain and overseas. The Stockwell College was built in 1861.

Lecture hall, Stockwell Training College, *c.* 1900. The board on the end wall carried the message 'seniors may go out this evening provided they are not wanted by the supervisor (but please . . . return by 8pm)'.

Stockwell College School, *c.* 1900. Attached to the college, on the right in the view opposite, was a school where the trainee teachers were able to practise. In the 1920s it accommodated around 700 children. This view shows the class known as the 7th standard. The college moved out of London in 1935, and the building was demolished and replaced by blocks of flats.

Stockwell Green, 1874. This open space, the historic centre of Stockwell, was still unfenced in the mid-nineteenth century. However, building began a couple of years after this photograph was taken, and soon covered the entire area.

Landor Road, looking past the corner of Hargwyne Street on the right, *c.* 1914. In the distance can be seen the spire of St Andrew's Church, whose present building dates from 1867. Ironically, the undertakers' business on the right was almost next to the gate of the South Western Hospital.

Landor Road, looking past the corner of Arlesford Road, *c.* 1914. The barber's shop on the left, advertising private warm baths for 6*d*, would have been providing a useful service for households without a bathroom.

Landor Road, looking past the corner of Hubert Grove on the right, *c*. 1914. The photographer evidently worked his way along this major shopping thoroughfare, taking a series of attractive views, all of which have been included here.

Landor Road, looking past the corner of Tasman Road on the right, *c*. 1914. The German-sounding name of the baker's shop on the corner disappeared shortly afterwards, a common occurrence during the First World War.

The entrance gates to the South Western Hospital, Landor Road, *c*. 1914. This was opened in 1871 as the South Western Fever Hospital, specifically to cater for fever and smallpox patients. Later it dealt also with tuberculosis and other infectious diseases. The large group of buildings extended from Landor Road to Pulross Road.

South Western Hospital, *c*. 1922. A children's playground with swings was provided. The hospital was used for air-raid casualties in the Second World War, but suffered bomb damage, particularly to a newly built isolation block.

South Western Hospital, *c.* 1922. A number of nurses can be seen looking out of the windows. The hospital subsequently came into more general use, including acute medical and surgical and geriatric cases, and out-patients.

South Western Hospital, *c.* 1922. The people in this view appear to be kitchen staff. The majority of the buildings were demolished in the early 1990s and what remains now serves as the headquarters of the West Lambeth Community Care (NHS) Trust.

Landor Road, looking past the corner of Willington Road on the right, *c.* 1914. The Avondale Hall was advertised as a venue for music and dancing.

Landor Road, looking from a point near the Clapham Road end, *c.* 1914. One of the most striking features of this series of views is the number of people simply standing around in the middle of the road, such was the absence of motor traffic.

Tasman Road, looking past the junction with Andalus Road, towards Landor Road, *c.* 1914. Originally Andalus Road continued across Tasman Road here and through to Willington Road. Note the matching pair of wine merchants' premises on the opposite corners.

Bomb-site in Rhodesia Road, July 1944. Members of the Home Guard, mostly officers apparently, are being given instructions by a Civil Defence warden, using a rather basic form of public address system. Not all seem to be paying attention!

Clapham Road, looking towards the corner of Jeffreys Road, *c.* 1930. On the left was the imposing front of Trinity Presbyterian Church, dating from 1862 but demolished (and not rebuilt) in the 1950s. Further along is a garage, where a row of petrol pumps and an AA sign are just visible. Beyond these can be seen the roof of St Augustine's Church.

Jeffreys Road, looking from the corner of Clapham Road, *c.* 1912. On the left is St Augustine's Church; the building, dating from 1899, ceased to be used as a church in its own right in 1950 and became the parish hall of St John's Church, which stands further along Clapham Road. Much of Jeffreys Road suffered damage during the Second World War and has been rebuilt.

Jeffreys Road, looking past the corner of Bromfelde Road, *c.* 1912. Originally Bromfelde Road ran from beyond Union Road right through to this point; much of the road has disappeared in a housing development, but a short portion leading off Jeffreys Road here remains as a cul-de-sac, renamed McCall Close.

Clapham Maternity Hospital, on the corner of Jeffreys Road and Bromfelde Road, *c.* 1900. This was founded in 1889 by the pioneer woman doctor and obstetrician Annie McCall. A believer in the importance of ante-natal care and natural childbirth, she achieved a very low maternal mortality rate. A major extension was built at the rear in 1914, and the older front part was bombed in the Second World War. The hospital closed in 1970, and the building was used as a health centre for a while.

Jeffreys Road, looking past the corner of Clarence Street (later renamed Clarence Walk), *c.* 1912. Much of this side of the road was reconstructed with blocks of flats in the 1950s.

Paradise Road, *c.* 1912. Originally this road ran entirely straight between Clapham Road and Larkhall Lane, parallel with Jeffreys Road. Severely damaged in the Second World War, its line was much altered when the large 1950s estate of blocks of flats was built.

Studley Road, *c*. 1912. Originally this road also ran straight between Clapham Road and Larkhall Lane, parallel with Paradise Road. It too had its line altered in the post-war reconstruction of this widely bomb-damaged area.

Bomb damage in Studley Road, 25 June 1944. Beyond the wreckage can be seen the Methodist church. The large brick structures along the side of the road were public air-raid shelters.

Clapham Road, looking past the corner of Paradise Road on the left, *c*. 1930. As well as the residential streets behind, this row of shops on the main road was also redeveloped in the 1950s. The war memorial can just be seen in the distance.

Binfield Road, looking towards Clapham Road, *c*. 1912. This is another road that was completely rebuilt with blocks of flats in the 1950s.

Binfield Road, looking in the opposite direction, *c.* 1930. A notable post-war building nearby is Stockwell bus garage; at the time of its construction in 1952 it possessed the largest clear roof span (with no intermediate support) in Europe.

Binfield Institute, on the corner of Lansdowne Road (later Lansdowne Way) and Binfield Road, *c.* 1915. The line of Binfield Road has since been altered; the corner in this view was adjacent to the end of Larkhall Lane. The notice-board advertised a young men's institute and club, open weekday evenings and Saturdays, and a Sunday school.

Priory Grove, looking from near the Larkhall Lane end, *c.* 1912. Much of the western side of this rather quaint narrow street has been demolished in the process of forming Larkhall Park.

Priory Grove, looking towards the corner of Priory Mews, *c.* 1912. In the distance can be seen the characteristic architecture of an LCC school.

CLAPHAM

*Park Court, Clapham Park Road, near the corner of
Abbeville Road, c. 1914. This attractively decorated
block of flats was built in the early 1900s. Note the old-
fashioned sign-post around which the children are
playing.*

Clapham High Street, looking past the corner of Cato Road, *c.* 1914. The Electric Pavilion cinema and the Clapham Public Hall, occupying the block between the corners of Aristotle Road and Cato Road, had both opened around 1911/12.

A science class at Aristotle Road School, *c.* 1910. It is most interesting to see this early example of a girls' science class at work in the laboratory.

Looking from Clapham Road across the junction with Bedford Road and Landor Road, *c.* 1914. Note the horse drinking from a trough while the passengers in its carriage wait.

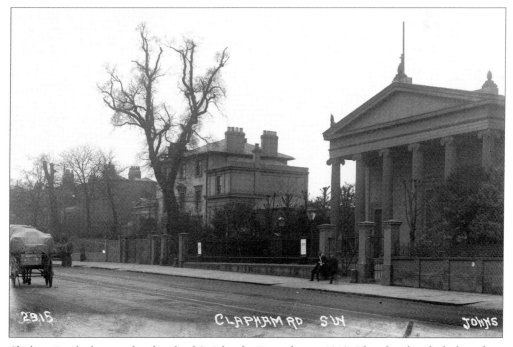

Clapham Road, showing the church of St John the Evangelist, *c.* 1912. This church, which dates from 1842, still stands but the houses to the left were replaced by blocks of flats in the 1950s.

Gaskell Road, looking from a point near the original Larkhall Lane end, *c.* 1912. In a major housing development in the 1970s, the road layout in this area was considerably altered. Only the southern portion of Gaskell Road remains, as a cul-de-sac off Union Road, and all the old cottage terraces have been demolished.

Union Street, *c.* 1912. This little street originally extended between Larkhall Lane and Bromfelde Road, in line with Smedley Street; later it was incorporated into Smedley Street, but only a short portion now remains as a cul-de-sac off Larkhall Lane. All the old cottages, much war-damaged, have been cleared.

Union Road, just beyond the junction with Bromfelde Road, looking towards Larkhall Lane, *c.* 1914. The houses on the right were bombed in the Second World War, and prefabs stood here for over twenty years before new housing was completed.

Albion Road (later renamed Albion Avenue), *c.* 1914. This road was entirely redeveloped with blocks of flats in the 1930s.

Southville (now vanished), *c.* 1912. This road of small villas and cottages ran from Wandsworth Road to meet Larkhall Lane at its junction with Priory Grove. At one time marking the Lambeth borough boundary, the road disappeared with the formation of Larkhall Park over an area of demolished housing in the 1970s.

Clifton Street (later renamed Courland Street, now vanished), *c.* 1912. This street also ran between Wandsworth Road and Larkhall Lane, parallel with Southville, and it has similarly disappeared under Larkhall Park.

Wandsworth Road, looking past the corner of Albion Road (later Albion Avenue) on the right, *c.* 1914. On the left was the Clapham Constitutional Club.

Wandsworth Road, looking past the corner of Brayburne Avenue, *c.* 1914. The South London Line from Victoria to London Bridge, passing through Wandsworth Road station, was the earliest above-ground railway in London to be electrified, a 6,600 volts AC overhead wire system being installed in 1909. On the left can be seen one of the gantries supporting the wires.

Wandsworth Road, showing the same location as in the previous picture but viewed from a different angle, *c.* 1914. The buildings on the left have been cleared as part of a major redevelopment.

Wandsworth Road, looking past the corner of Westbury Street on the right, *c.* 1914. This area, adjacent to the location in the top view, was redeveloped with blocks of flats in the 1960s.

W.H. Gardner's weighing machine and cutting implement shop, Wandsworth Road, *c.* 1910. Note the model figure with a sword and scales over the frontage.

Cedars Road, looking from near the Wandsworth Road end, *c.* 1914. Behind the houses can just be seen the tower of St Saviour's Church, which was destroyed by bombing in 1940 and not rebuilt. Almost all the large villas in this road were demolished for a 1960s housing development, which also covered the site of the church.

Clapham Common North Side, looking past the corner of Wix's Lane, *c.* 1914. The ornate railings have not survived. Wix's Lane now marks the Lambeth borough boundary.

Clapham Common North Side, looking towards the corner of Orlando Road, *c.* 1914. On the extreme right the Clapham public library, built in 1889, is just visible. The large house with the dome adjacent to the library was demolished about 1916, and an optical factory was built on its site. The factory building has in turn been converted to Lambeth Council offices.

The Polygon, *c.* 1914. This unique island block of buildings, facing the north end of Clapham Common, dates from the late eighteenth century, and survives despite suffering considerable damage in the Second World War. Some of the products in the advertisements are still household names.

Bromells Road, looking towards the junction with Venn Street, *c.* 1914. On the extreme right was the large premises of an ironmonger and builders' merchant.

S.F. Stevens' bakery and tea shop, The Pavement, *c.* 1910. The notices in the window illustrate the prices: a pot of tea, roll and butter cost 5*d*, while mince pies were seven for 1*s*.

Venn Street, looking from the Clapham High Street end, *c.* 1914. Noting the prices in the window again, gent's haircutting was available for 4*d*.

Looking from Venn Street towards the junction of Clapham High Street and Clapham Park Road, *c.* 1914. The Electric Palace cinema on the right had opened about 1910. In the centre of the view is St Mary's Roman Catholic Church, dating from 1851, to which was later added a monastery; both still survive.

Clapham Park Road, looking past the corner of St Alphonsus Road on the right, *c.* 1914. Only a few of the small, original buildings survive in this road.

Clapham Park Road, looking past the corner of Holwood Place on the right, *c.* 1914. The corner shop on the left, selling household goods, claimed 'we are the cheapest oilmen in London'. The area on the left, around Park Crescent (later renamed Clapham Crescent), was rebuilt with a large estate of blocks of flats in the 1950s.

Clapham Park Road, looking from the sharp bend in the road towards the Clapham High Street end, *c.* 1914. Most of the remainder of this road was redeveloped in the 1980s.

Clapham Park Road, showing the buildings opposite to the row of shops in the foreground of the view above, *c.* 1914. On the extreme left can be seen the large Edwardian block of flats, Park Court.

Park Hill, looking north, *c.* 1914. In this semi-rural scene, the tower of St James's Church is just visible behind the trees on the left. The building of 1870 was bombed in the Second World War; a new church was opened in 1958 on the original site, but fronting on to Briarwood Road.

The 5th Clapham (Holy Trinity) Scout Troop, *c.* 1914. The exact location of this view is not known, but is presumably not far from Holy Trinity Church, Clapham Common.

Clapham Common South Side, looking towards the junction with Clapham High Street and Clapham Park Road, c. 1914. The underground City & South London Railway was extended beyond Stockwell to Clapham Common in 1900, and the original station building on the corner of Clapham Park Road can just be picked out in the distance.

Clapham Common South Side, looking past the corner of Windmill Drive on the left, c. 1914. The nearest building on the right was the Clapham High School for Girls, dating from 1903. Used for other schools in later years, it was demolished and replaced by housing in the 1980s.

Clapham Common South Side, looking past the corner of Lynette Avenue, *c.* 1914. Relatively little traffic appears on this main thoroughfare.

S.C. Grimmond's bakery and tea shop on the corner of Clapham Common South Side and Narbonne Avenue, *c.* 1905. The prices quoted in the window for wedding and birthday cakes range from 5*s* to £5 5*s*.

South London Hospital for Women, Clapham Common South Side, *c*. 1935. This was opened in 1916, and a major extension was built in 1935. The notice-board announced that the hospital was 'for the treatment of women and children by medical women, and was supported by voluntary contributions.'

A children's ward in South London Hospital for Women, *c*. 1935. The name plate on the wall over the nearest bed presumably commemorated a donor. The hospital closed in the 1980s.

ACKNOWLEDGEMENTS

All the pictures in this book come from the collections held by Lambeth Archives Department. The following belong to the Sid Hayden Collection (both pictures on a page unless otherwise stated): pages 43, 45 (lower), 46, 47, 48, 49, 50, 51 (lower), 53 (lower), 54, 55 (upper), 57, 58, 59, 60, 61, 62 (lower), 63, 65, 66 (lower), 67, 68 (upper), 69 (upper), 70, 72 (lower), 73, 74, 75, 76, 77, 78 (upper), 83 (lower), 84 (upper). The following pictures belong to the Ron Elam Collection: 30 (upper), 35 (lower), 36 (upper), 37 (upper), 45 (upper), 84 (lower), 92 (lower), 93 (upper), 101 (lower), 105 (lower), 108 (lower), 115, 118 (lower), 122 (lower), 124 (lower), 125 (lower).

This book has been researched using the extensive holdings of Lambeth Archives Department; the helpful assistance of Jon Newman and Sue McKenzie, Lambeth Archivists, and all their staff is gratefully acknowledged. Much information about the photographer Strudwick and the exact locations of his pictures was kindly provided by Brian Bloice and George Young; and information about the collector Woolley was supplied by Patricia Jenkyns. A conducted tour of the Duchy of Cornwall estate by Nicholas Long was also very helpful. Most importantly, the book would not have been possible without the excellent work of Alan Robertson, who has produced from glass-plate and other negatives the majority of the prints (other than the Sid Hayden Collection) used in this book.

BRITAIN IN OLD PHOTOGRAPHS

berystwyth & North Ceredigion
round Abingdon
ton
derney: A Second Selection
ong the Avon from Stratford to
Tewkesbury
trincham
nersham
ound Amesbury
glesey
nold & Bestwood
nold & Bestwood: A Second
Selection
undel & the Arun Valley
hbourne
ound Ashby-de-la-Zouch
ro Aircraft
lesbury
ham & Tooting
nburyshire
nes, Mortlake & Sheen
nsley
h
aconsfield
lford
lfordshire at Work
lworth
erley
xley
eford
ston
mingham Railways
hop's Stortford &
awbridgeworth
hopstone & Seaford
hopstone & Seaford: A Second
election
ck Country Aviation
ck Country Railways
ck Country Road Transport
ckburn
ckpool
ound Blandford Forum
tchley
ton
rnemouth
dford
intree & Bocking at Work
con
ntwood
dgwater & the River Parrett
llington
lport & the Bride Valley
rley Hill
ghton & Hove
ghton & Hove: A Second
lection
tol
und Bristol
ton & Norwood
y Broadstairs & St Peters
mley, Keston & Hayes

Buckingham & District
Burford
Bury
Bushbury
Camberwell
Cambridge
Cannock Yesterday & Today
Canterbury: A Second Selection
Castle Combe to Malmesbury
Chadwell Heath
Chard & Ilminster
Chatham Dockyard
Chatham & Gillingham
Cheadle
Cheam & Belmont
Chelmsford
Cheltenham: A Second Selection
Cheltenham at War
Cheltenham in the 1950s
Chepstow & the River Wye
Chesham Yesterday & Today
Cheshire Railways
Chester
Chippenham & Lacock
Chiswick
Chorley & District
Cirencester
Around Cirencester
Clacton-on-Sea
Around Clitheroe
Clwyd Railways
Clydesdale
Colchester
Colchester 1940–70
Colyton & Seaton
The Cornish Coast
Corsham & Box
The North Cotswolds
Coventry: A Second Selection
Around Coventry
Cowes & East Cowes
Crawley New Town
Around Crawley
Crewkerne & the Ham Stone
Villages
Cromer
Croydon
Crystal Palace, Penge & Anerley
Darlington
Darlington: A Second Selection
Dawlish & Teignmouth
Deal
Derby
Around Devizes
Devon Aerodromes
East Devon at War
Around Didcot & the Hagbournes
Dorchester
Douglas
Dumfries
Dundee at Work
Durham People

Durham at Work
Ealing & Northfields
East Grinstead
East Ham
Eastbourne
Elgin
Eltham
Ely
Enfield
Around Epsom
Esher
Evesham to Bredon
Exeter
Exmouth & Budleigh Salterton
Fairey Aircraft
Falmouth
Farnborough
Farnham: A Second Selection
Fleetwood
Folkestone: A Second Selection
Folkestone: A Third Selection
The Forest of Dean
Frome
Fulham
Galashiels
Garsington
Around Garstang
Around Gillingham
Gloucester
Gloucester: from the Walwin
Collection
North Gloucestershire at War
South Gloucestershire at War
Gosport
Goudhurst to Tenterden
Grantham
Gravesend
Around Gravesham
Around Grays
Great Yarmouth
Great Yarmouth: A Second
Selection
Greenwich & Woolwich
Grimsby
Around Grimsby
Grimsby Docks
Gwynedd Railways
Hackney: A Second Selection
Hackney: A Third Selection
From Haldon to Mid-Dartmoor
Hammersmith & Shepherds Bush
Hampstead to Primrose Hill
Harrow & Pinner
Hastings
Hastings: A Second Selection
Haverfordwest
Hayes & West Drayton
Around Haywards Heath
Around Heathfield
Around Heathfield: A Second
Selection
Around Helston

Around Henley-on-Thames
Herefordshire
Herne Bay
Heywood
The High Weald
The High Weald: A Second
Selection
Around Highworth
Around Highworth & Faringdon
Hitchin
Holderness
Honiton & the Otter Valley
Horsham & District
Houghton-le-Spring &
Hetton-le-Hole
Houghton-le-Spring & Hetton-le-
Hole: A Second Selection
Huddersfield: A Second Selection
Huddersfield: A Third Selection
Ilford
Ilfracombe
Ipswich: A Second Selection
Islington
Jersey: A Third Selection
Kendal
Kensington & Chelsea
East Kent at War
Keswick & the Central Lakes
Around Keynsham & Saltford
The Changing Face of Keynsham
Kingsbridge
Kingston
Kinver
Kirkby & District
Kirkby Lonsdale
Around Kirkham
Knowle & Dorridge
The Lake Counties at Work
Lancashire
The Lancashire Coast
Lancashire North of the Sands
Lancashire Railways
East Lancashire at War
Around Lancaster
Lancing & Sompting
Around Leamington Spa
Around Leamington Spa:
A Second Selection
Leeds in the News
Leeds Road & Rail
Around Leek
Leicester
The Changing Face of Leicester
Leicester at Work
Leicestershire People
Around Leighton Buzzard &
Linslade
Letchworth
Lewes
Lewisham & Deptford:
A Second Selection
Lichfield

Lincoln
Lincoln Cathedral
The Lincolnshire Coast
Liverpool
Around Llandudno
Around Lochaber
Theatrical London
Around Louth
The Lower Fal Estuary
Lowestoft
Luton
Lympne Airfield
Lytham St Annes
Maidenhead
Around Maidenhead
Around Malvern
Manchester
Manchester Road & Rail
Mansfield
Marlborough: A Second Selection
Marylebone & Paddington
Around Matlock
Melton Mowbray
Around Melksham
The Mendips
Merton & Morden
Middlesbrough
Midsomer Norton & Radstock
Around Mildenhall
Milton Keynes
Minehead
Monmouth & the River Wye
The Nadder Valley
Newark
Around Newark
Newbury
Newport, Isle of Wight
The Norfolk Broads
Norfolk at War
North Fylde
North Lambeth
North Walsham & District
Northallerton
Northampton
Around Norwich
Nottingham 1944–74
The Changing Face of Nottingham
Victorian Nottingham
Nottingham Yesterday & Today
Nuneaton
Around Oakham
Ormskirk & District
Otley & District
Oxford: The University
Oxford Yesterday & Today
Oxfordshire Railways: A Second
   Selection
Oxfordshire at School
Around Padstow
Pattingham & Wombourne

Penwith
Penzance & Newlyn
Around Pershore
Around Plymouth
Poole
Portsmouth
Poulton le Fylde
Preston
Prestwich
Pudsey
Radcliffe
RAF Chivenor
RAF Cosford
RAF Hawkinge
RAF Manston
RAF Manston: A Second Selection
RAF St Mawgan
RAF Tangmere
Ramsgate & Thanet Life
Reading
Reading: A Second Selection
Redditch & the Needle District
Redditch: A Second Selection
Richmond, Surrey
Rickmansworth
Around Ripley
The River Soar
Romney Marsh
Romney Marsh: A Second
   Selection
Rossendale
Around Rotherham
Rugby
Around Rugeley
Ruislip
Around Ryde
St Albans
St Andrews
Salford
Salisbury
Salisbury: A Second Selection
Salisbury: A Third Selection
Around Salisbury
Sandhurst & Crowthorne
Sandown & Shanklin
Sandwich
Scarborough
Scunthorpe
Seaton, Lyme Regis & Axminster
Around Seaton & Sidmouth
Sedgley & District
The Severn Vale
Sherwood Forest
Shrewsbury
Shrewsbury: A Second Selection
Shropshire Railways
Skegness
Around Skegness
Skipton & the Dales
Around Slough

Smethwick
Somerton & Langport
Southampton
Southend-on-Sea
Southport
Southwark
Southwell
Southwold to Aldeburgh
Stafford
Around Stafford
Staffordshire Railways
Around Staveley
Stepney
Stevenage
The History of Stilton Cheese
Stoke-on-Trent
Stoke Newington
Stonehouse to Painswick
Around Stony Stratford
Around Stony Stratford: A Second
   Selection
Stowmarket
Streatham
Stroud & the Five Valleys
Stroud & the Five Valleys: A
   Second Selection
Stroud's Golden Valley
The Stroudwater and Thames &
   Severn Canals
The Stroudwater and Thames &
   Severn Canals: A Second
   Selection
Suffolk at Work
Suffolk at Work: A Second
   Selection
The Heart of Suffolk
Sunderland
Sutton
Swansea
Swindon: A Third Selection
Swindon: A Fifth Selection
Around Tamworth
Taunton
Around Taunton
Teesdale
Teesdale: A Second Selection
Tenbury Wells
Around Tettenhall & Codshall
Tewkesbury & the Vale of
   Gloucester
Thame to Watlington
Around Thatcham
Around Thirsk
Thornbury to Berkeley
Tipton
Around Tonbridge
Trowbridge
Around Truro
TT Races
Tunbridge Wells

Tunbridge Wells: A Second
   Selection
Twickenham
Uley, Dursley & Cam
The Upper Fal
The Upper Tywi Valley
Uxbridge, Hillingdon & Cowley
The Vale of Belvoir
The Vale of Conway
Ventnor
Wakefield
Wallingford
Walsall
Waltham Abbey
Wandsworth at War
Wantage, Faringdon & the Vale
   Villages
Around Warwick
Weardale
Weardale: A Second Selection
Wednesbury
Wells
Welshpool
West Bromwich
West Wight
Weston-super-Mare
Around Weston-super-Mare
Weymouth & Portland
Around Wheatley
Around Whetstone
Whitchurch to Market Drayton
Around Whitstable
Wigton & the Solway Plain
Willesden
Around Wilton
Wimbledon
Around Windsor
Wingham, Addisham &
   Littlebourne
Wisbech
Witham & District
Witney
Around Witney
The Witney District
Wokingham
Around Woodbridge
Around Woodstock
Woolwich
Woolwich Royal Arsenal
Around Wootton Bassett,
   Cricklade & Purton
Worcester
Worcester in a Day
Around Worcester
Worcestershire at Work
Around Worthing
Wotton-under-Edge to Chippin
   Sodbury
Wymondham & Attleborough
The Yorkshire Wolds

To order any of these titles please telephone our distributor, Littlehampton Book Services on 01903 72159
For a catalogue of these and our other titles please ring Regina Schinner on 01453 731114